Cages to Stages

How S.T.E.M. Changed My Life

Antoine "TK" Patton

Antoine "TK" Patton

ISBN:
978-0-692-17328-2

DEDICATION

This is dedicated to the people who are so poor that the top of the Section 8 list is a milestone.

This is dedicated to the people so content, that not enough is almost plenty.

This is dedicated to people who have been slept on so much they can see other people's dreams more vivid than their own.

This is especially dedicated to the children of the United States of America who have been underexposed to opportunities that others are beginning to take for granted.

This is especially, especially dedicated to the women. I'm referring to the core of every single one of you. This world would have been soulless by now if it had not been for your existence, your sacrifices, your strength, your nurturing and your belief in boys and men like me.
To name a few of you: G-Baby, Mommy (Brownie), Momma Dukes, Mom, Nana, Gina (Queena), Tay-Tay, Ri, Tiffany, Auntie Monie, Auntie Niecy, Auntie Vee, Auntie Glenda, Soap Soap aka R.O, Tizzy, Lina, Jazz, Chante`, Caiya, Nneka, Laura, Paola, Chantla, Sasha, India, Anita, CoCo Loco Marissa, Marissa G., Tima, Nicole, Sade, Mrs. Patterson, Mrs. White, Sweet Mary, Auntie Crystal, Auntie Crystal S., Wanda, Jazz, Tubby, Roxanne, Ms. Tyson, Lauren and last but not least, two incipient but promising stars of our future: Jay & Nova.

I've done a lot of bad things in my past. Way too many. So to the people I have disrespected, offended or hurt, and who I may never get a chance to see in person ever again, I want to use this time to say how much I sincerely apologize for what I may have done to you or any of your loved ones. I was in a dark place of my life between the ages of 15 and 20. On the day I graduated from 8th grade, I witnessed two men rob my mother and newborn twin sisters at gunpoint in our home. They threw one of my sisters onto the ground, head first. I never had a chance to confront those guys. So I can imagine how some of the people I have negatively impacted must feel. I don't have too much pride to beg for forgiveness. That is how much being known as a respectable man means to me.

CONTENTS

ACKNOWLEDGMENTS

Thank you to my immediate family for being patient with me as I put what seemed like endless hours into writing, and re-writing this book.

Thank you to my brother for Zach inspiring me to create the cover for this book and thank you for designing the Unlock Box and the Cages to Stages Album designs.

Thank you to my editor Intelligent Allah.

Thank you to my partners, sounding board and Cages to Stages Brothers: Greg, Craig, Tink, Boy and R.O.

Thank you to all of the brothers, some of whom I speak about in this book, who encouraged me to stay focused and not recidivate.

Thank you to my good friend Life who introduced me to mediation. Without it, I would not have been able to stay focused and complete this book.

Thank you to my good friend P aka Amir for making sure I kept music a priority in my life.

Thank you to all of the teachers and volunteers who have went into prison to teach me or any prisoner. I know most of you were getting paid, but it wasn't about the paycheck. I appreciate you all for believing in individuals who most of society has erased from their memory.

If you're not living the best life you can be living, meaning you're not growing, you're not happy and you're not spreading positivity, you're in a Cage.

If you're living the best life you can be living, meaning you're growing, you're happy and you're spreading positivity, you're on a Stage.

INTRODUCTION

People get pumped when I tell them I went from Cages 2 Stages. They know it's true and they know it must have been hard. Many have used the word "impressed." And I sometimes just smirk because I used to be in the business of impressing people: my peers, my cousins, younger siblings, the cute girls in high school and many more. I'm now in a new business: inspiration. Trying to impress people had me hanging and slanging on the same old avenues instead of creating new avenues.

I can condense this short book into two powerful words: Know Thyself. This book is about self-awareness—principally, those exact moments of being most self-aware. It's so easy to get caught up in the world to the point that we forget whose analysis of us matters most. I appreciate the opinion of my mother, my father, my friends and even my social network critics. But until I started asking myself (through literally asking myself), I was lacking the most important opinion. As the great Lauryn Hill so beautifully said during her MTV Unplugged live show, "Whenever we submit our will to someone else's opinion, a part of us dies."

I went to prison and yes, some would consider that a Cage. But the Cages I am really referring to are the mental Cages we are unconsciously and sometimes involuntarily locked in. It's crazy because you don't realize that you're in a Cage until the moment you get out of the Cage. I'll say that again - you don't realize that you're in a Cage until the moment you get out of the Cage.

I'll give an example. Let's say your job is a Cage—meaning your job itself or someone at your job can be given credit as one of the things stopping you from reaching your best life. If you're not living the best life you can be living. Meaning you're not growing, you're not happy and you're not spreading positivity. You're in a Cage.

You hate working at a fast-food restaurant and you'd rather be a dentist or instead of being a cashier you'd rather be the shift manager. At the end of the day, where there's a will there's a way. So the moment you realize you don't have to stay in the fast-food industry forever, you start formulating thoughts, decisions and actions that lead you towards what you really want to do. As you intentionally and consistently make the right thoughts, decisions and actions, the wheels in your life are turning. You may be trapped at the moment, but at least now you're slowly but surely turning the key that is unlocking your Cage. As long as you continue intentionally thinking, deciding and acting, you're out of your Cage. Just don't be that person who turns around and locks himself back in the Cage. Like the old me.

My mental Cages spun out of control until they finally evolved into physical Cages. I went to prison in 2008 for eight years. Growing up as an impressionable teenager in Buffalo, NY, I had gained an addiction to guns, which are abnormally abundant in the urban community. After my apartment was burglarized in 2006, twice might I add, I took the term "overprotective" to a new level. I was famous for double-checking and triple-checking everything. Always double counting my money. Always checking up on my family who lived in the heart of the hood. And I was always checking on the streets to see what my clout level was. Somebody had robbed me and I had no idea who. I share vivid details about this experience on "Hubris," a song I wrote on my Cages to Stages album.

I remember not trusting many people after that. I lived through my rearview. My favorite gun at that time was a worn black and brown .357 magnum revolver. I took it everywhere with me. I drove around with it in the soccer mom van I was driving at that time. I had it in my jeans while I played dice at the park with the neighborhood boys. I admit that it was over the top at times, but I also admit that when I was in danger, it saved my life.
Ironically enough, the .357 is what landed me in prison for a majority of my 20s. In New York State, you can get anywhere between three and 15 years for criminal possession of a weapon. On July 11th, 2008 it was decided that my lucky number was eight. Not even 21 yet, and I was about to serve eight years in prison. I just knew my life was over.

Nothing good came out of prison for me. The system just isn't setup that way. It's what I created in prison that helped me blossom. It was intentionally unlocking my Cages which lead me to the Stages I'm on today—Stages being the platforms, experiences and moments through which I am living my best life. If you're living the best life you can be living, meaning you're growing, you're happy and you're spreading positivity, then you're on a Stage.

I ended up executing something the penal system would have never expected. I transformed every cell they put me in into a think tank and a meditation factory. It's what I sometimes liked to call it a metaphorical "S.T.E.M. cell," because like the stem cells in our body, I was regenerating life (my very own) from within a cell. My goal was to master solitude, seclusion and in the process, self.

Okay, maybe I went too far with the mastering-the-self-thing, but I am no longer a novice when it comes to knowing who I am. This is the essence of my life changing. So please keep in mind, when I say "S.T.E.M. Changed My Life" Don't mistake that for S.T.E.M. has changed me. My motto is, "Don't become, recognize what already is," Our potential is always there, but our lives—our days, our nights, our obligations, our desires, our fragile humanity—is what takes us in the opposite direction.

The level of thinking and analysis that comes with thinking through S.T.E.M. concepts, slowly but surely leaked into the thinking and analysis I did of myself. If I can quote the legend Lauryn's MTV Unplugged performance one more time, "I became one of those mad scientists who does the test on themselves first, you see, to make sure that they work…I'm not going to give you something I haven't tried and tested for myself."

Learning S.T.E.M. topics helped me recognize that I never had a skill problem, I had a will problem. Understanding me (that inside of me) is what changed my life (that outside of me). I went from seeing myself as a hustler, rapper, player and G, to a creative business man, musician, an accountable friend and proud father. To you who have known me some time, you still do. I haven't changed, only my perception has. I'm hopeful that this book will inspire a couple people to boldly strive to do some intensive introspection. As contradicting as it may sound, there is great power in knowing how much you don't know about yourself.

Technology

Woodbourne Correctional Facility
February 19, 2011

I have been bounced around to multiple jails and prisons. Woodbourne was by far the smallest. There were about 800 prisoners and 200 staff including prison guards, GED teachers and other administration. In 2010 I was moved to Woodbourne because while in Elmira Correctional Facility I applied for a Liberal Arts college program ran and supported by Bard College. After about two weeks I found out I was accepted. Out of 1500 Elmira prisoners, about 400 applied for the college program. Out of the 400 applicants only 15 were accepted.

We were tested by writing an essay based on prompts the college staff gave us. I remember I wrote about George Orwell's 'Shooting an Elephant". In the story, a Burma police officer is called upon to shoot a wild elephant. Against his better judgement he does shoot the elephant and has to watch it die a slow and painful death. I compared the peer pressure the police officer dealt with to the peer pressure youth deal with when they join gangs. Sometimes you do the worst things because you are seeking the best things: love, solidarity, family. The college staff loved my essay.

After about two semesters in Elmira, I was told it was time to move to Woodbourne; that was the only way to get the Associates degree. I knew family visits would slow down because I would be six hours away from my Buffalo, NY family. But I knew it would be worth the sacrifice especially since if I earned the Associates degree the Department of Corrections would subtract six months from my sentence. Sounded like a no-brainer to me and my family.

The ride from Elmira to Woodbourne was three hours long. A 23-year-old guy named Brandon was shackled to my my right foot and my right hand. Ironically, he would become my right-hand man.

He too was in the college program but him and I never spoke in Elmira. On that prison bus, we found out we had plenty to talk about. He was from Rochester, NY which is Buffalo's twin city. They are about 30 minutes apart. We were the same age, had the same passion for music, both were eager for higher education and we both wanted something different from the street life we used to live. We went from giving each other subtle head nods in Elmira to being best friends in Woodbourne. We hung together so much people thought we were brothers. Unfortunately, we also ended up in the "hole" together.

I couldn't believe it. I had messed up again. Already serving eight years of my life, I managed to get myself "double-incarcerated." The prison guards at Woodbourne put me under what is called "keep-lock" status, short for: keep his cell locked all day. Actually, 24 hours in a cell is illegal - they had to let us get at least 1 hour of recreational time. So keep his cell locked for 23 hours.

As I sat on the cushionless bed, I was confounded. I was sure I had changed: I was enrolled in a very resourceful and challenging college-in-prison program. I was keeping a journal to track my mental and spiritual progress; and of course, I was exercising regularly becoming more health conscious like most prisoners do. But one thing I remember from being 23 years old, I still lacked purposeful direction.

Even though I was in college while incarcerated, I hadn't thought of a way to turn the liberal arts degree I would soon attain into something tangible. I was definitely thinking more critically now that I had taken higher education more seriously, but I was really missing that old entrepreneurial side of me. There's something to be said about the street hustler who goes to prison and doesn't have an outlet to express and improve his or her entrepreneurism. How was learning about the exuberance of King Louis XVI in my HIST 327 class going to put me in a better position to become a provider upon release?

Nagging questions like this were difficult to answer, so after I wrote the 10-page paper about the King's luxurious and irresponsible reign, then completed my daily dose of push-ups, pull-ups and dips, Brandon and I would sit idle pondering our future. We would pull out our black and white composition notebooks and strategize on building profit and not-for-profit corporations.

Good ideas would come, bad ideas come. Either way, it was all theory. I call it the Prison Bell Theory. I'll help you understand. First, visualize a bell in your head. See how it curves up, reaches its high point, and then goes back down like a mountainside? That is the journey of the prisoner's potential. You work hard to think better, eat better and act better, but there's only so much you can do before the prison handbook slaps you with a hundred rules and regulations for why you can't do just about anything citizens on the outside are doing. But as the 13th Amendment clearly states, my crime is a justification for slavery.

Without an entrepreneurial outlet, Brandon and I would eventually become bored. And boredom, as the saying goes, is the devil's playground. I'm perceptive enough now to know that moments like these are what led me to being "double-incarcerated." As I sat in solitary confinement I wondered if I was the George Orwell's police officer - making bad decisions for good reasons - or the elephant - dying a slow and painful death. Or maybe I was both?

Brandon had a "great idea" and I once again was wrapped up in peer pressure cycle. He was the first person who saw the chemist in me. He wanted to get saucy (intoxicated) before the talent show we were going to perform at. He gassed me up to learn how to make jailhouse liquor. I did my jailhouse research and got a jailhouse plan together.

Making jailhouse liquor is about a five day process. Unfortunately, for us, four days in and the prison guards searched Brandon's "bunk" only to find a gallon worth of what we called "hooch." Because Brandon and I were known associates, the guards immediately searched my bunk next. Only thing they could find to connect me to the liquor was a pack of oatmeal with raisins missing out of it.

"Yes, raisins are a key ingredient to hooch, but I also sometimes just eat the raisins out of the oatmeal pack," is what I wanted to say. But I saved my breath.

I knew I was wrong, but I felt like the victim since I didn't have any liquor in my possession when they searched my quarters. Nonetheless, I ended up "keep-locked" for 14 days while Brandon took most of the weight and was sentenced to 60 days in "the box." Keep-lock isn't as severe as being in "the box," although in either case you're locked in a cell all day long with not much human contact and an inhumane lack of nutritious meals.

Miraculously, those two weeks are credited with disrupting my prior thinking patterns. It started with me facing the truth and owning up to the role I played in putting myself in yet another degrading position. Taking responsibility made me realize that I still had a lot of work to do, namely: increase my self-discipline, sharpen my decision-making skills, and start working towards some actual goals. Keep-locked for 23-hours a day, I began to pray five times a day (no, I wasn't Muslim). Eyes closed, I would sometimes just focus my thoughts for extended periods of time (no, I wasn't Buddhist). But what I did more than anything else was read, greedily (yes, I was hungry—in more ways than one).

I will always remember those days. A Latino friend of mine, Jay, would habitually sneak two-or-three-day-old Wall Street Journal and USA Today newspapers into the cell I was in. I fell in love and mostly anticipated the tech articles. The words, numbers, data and potential that I read about in those publications put a sort of fire in my body. I soon began to associate that fire with passion. I became passionate about entering the tech-industry. Finally, I thought to myself, I've found some solid direction. I was locked in the cell for 23 hours a day, but my imagination was on the moon.

This was in 2010. The phrase "there's an app for that" wasn't even a thing yet. But it wasn't far away. Every article was either about growth, the need for more innovation, or the potential to grow by being innovative. And if you didn't want to build your own app, there were more jobs than there were programmers. I wanted in.

To be clear, the only reason why it was halfway realistic for me to think I could get "in" was because I actually had the opportunity (access to a computer laboratory and software thanks to the college-in-prison program) and time (a bunch of time thanks to my addiction to guns). It was like walking by an interesting looking castle, and the front door is wide open...I was young enough, naive enough and risky enough to let my curiosity lead me inside.

In hindsight, I must have been motivated beyond the word itself. Stuck in that cell, I truly had no idea what programming was. Ironically, one month earlier, the college-in-prison program I was enrolled in had just brought a web development course to the facility. Unfortunately, I didn't sign up for that class because I was trapped in the mental Cage that coding, culturally speaking, was for nerds, let alone the type of intellect it must take. But like I said, I was working on extinguishing my tired ways of thinking.

When I began brainstorming ideas that I thought to be unique (i.e., a website/app where songwriters, and producers could auction off their work), I became even more committed to learning how to code.

"I have to bring my creations to life," I would tell myself.

I had changed my habits before and had even considered those changes milestones. But when you change how you think, well now, you are altering your destiny. I vowed to myself that if I was allowed to stay in this particular prison where the college program was being offered I would pick up a book and learn how to program software. Prisoners were often transferred to a different prison after a "keep-lock" incident. The prison staff weren't big fans of the college-in-prison program. We were getting serious accredited degrees — Associates and Bachelor degrees — for free. Between the challenging professors that came in to teach us and the antagonistic guards who came in to hassle us, I don't know how we got those degrees.

The universe ultimately accepted my vow. After my keep-lock time was served, I was able to stay in the prison and continue my college experience. I remember rushing to the in-prison computer lab. I wanted to see if any books were left hanging around. I'm here to remind you, speaking things into existence really works. I looked around in the computer lab, flipping books over and finally I found one, the only one left. It wasn't a programming software book, however, but the book did teach how to develop websites. Funny thing is, back then I didn't know the difference. So I put just as much enthusiasm into learning "client-side" languages like HTML, CSS, and JavaScript.

I got really good at coding, really fast. I attest that to dedication. It was painful. It was confusing. But it was like nothing I had ever done in my life. I had never been on the computer that much in my life so I found myself learning how that operates as well. I was teaching myself, but I had to balance that with my actual semester. I was taking 4 classes and learning how to code on the side.

I had access to the computers nine hours out of the day. Ninety-nine percent of students used the computer for typing papers for their classes. If I had a writing assignment due for one of my classes (e.g., a 10—15-page paper on Hegemony in Ireland), I would hand write the paper in the cell so that all my time in the computer lab could be devoted to coding.

Nothing had ever given me the adrenaline rush that I received while coding and debugging, not even the street life. While in prison, I often had nightmares about fake friends, funerals and an ugly fate. Poverty was always the back drop. But when I started staying up real late reading my web book, I would fall asleep dreaming about HTML tags and CSS selectors. Sometimes this would be annoying, but overall it was a relief compared to the alternative.

By the time Brandon was let out of "the box" 45 days later, I had taught myself the fundamentals of building websites. Not that it would have mattered, but he never once judged me by calling me a geek, nerd or lame. On the contrary, he too saw the opportunity in the tech industry so I began passing my knowledge and passion on to him. Brandon knew it, and I knew it: things were different.

Brandon was released from prison just 7 months later. I'll tell you how motivated Brandon was. Within three months of being released, he was enrolled into Rochester Institute of Technology, one of the top colleges in NY, pursuing his bachelor's degree in Computer and Information Sciences. I still had four more years left in prison. I saw it as four more years to sharpen up my programming skills. If Brandon was doing so well, I couldn't imagine where I would be in four years.

Technology changed my life.

Give me some grains, I'll turn it into gold/
Give me a Cage, I'll unlock the code/
Paid the price and kept it moving (uh)/
Treated that prison like a toll (uh)/
… Ex-Con now goals (huh?)/

"Cages" — Cages to Stages Album

ENGINEERING

Man I saw so much death/
All I know is Grieve and Grow/
And I went from Cages to Stages/
Feel like I'm dreaming bro/

"Half" —Cages to Stages Album

Most violence in prison doesn't stem from prisoner vs. guard conflict. Most violence in prison doesn't even stem from prisoner vs. prisoner conflict. No violence, in or outside of prison

for that matter, is more common than self-affliction. I witnessed people mentally torture themselves by continually fighting against their own consciences just to give off a false perception. If you play it right, you can get whatever you want in prison, whether you're a guard or a prisoner. But if someone perceives a crack in your armor, and decides to exploit it, you can die in prison, whether you're a guard or a prisoner. I didn't want a slice of prison power.

I didn't want to get attached to anything in prison. I wanted to survive and make it home. Regardless, some power came my way.

For the first two years I did my best to stay away from the spontaneous power-hungry "super-guards" and "super-gangsters." In the same instance, I was attracting them. When they approached me, however, they didn't bring conflict, they brought respect (though it took some time to understand exactly why).

It started with super-gangsters acknowledging me with subtle head nods and intense eye-contact. Not intimidating, more so recognition. Then a couple super-guards started calling me "General Patton" instead of my derogatory cell location number. "Hey twenty-one cell, you want to take a shower today?"

Then more super-gangsters began opening up to me about what books they had read and more super-guards asking about my plans when I leave prison. This interaction began taking place in the maximum-security prison I was housed in where tension is always thick and people keep their guards up. When I was transferred to a medium security prison, I began to understand the attention.

Many people say power only concedes to power. Slowly but surely, I was accumulating a limitless power of my own: knowledge. I was so busy analyzing the aura everyone else was projecting; I didn't stop to think what people thought of me. A couple years into my sentence I still looked 17. I wasn't in any of the GED classes since I had my H.S. diploma. And I read everything I could get my hands on: material on the money markets, real estate, non-profits and plenty of esoteric books. On the outside looking in, I was a good kid who made a bad mistake, when in fact I was a disruptive/destructive kid who made a full list of mistakes. But they didn't know that. To these super-guards and super-gangsters I still had "potential."

I didn't come to this conclusion myself. In the medium-security facility, people were much more outspoken. What I found interesting was how many people saw potential in me but not in themselves. These men, some 10, 20 and 30 years my senior, Black, White and Latino, had lost hope in themselves. Super-guards were complacent with going into a prison everyday even though they dreaded the redundancy of the job super-gangsters were back on their second and third bid, usually due to their expectations of themselves being so low that they limited their own opportunities and ended up caught in the revolving door. The prison and community supervision system are very easy to get into, but impossible to get out of.

When I finally became aware of all this (which I'll explain in a moment), I became hungrier. I too had suffered from this mental incarceration for a period of my life. Scared to expect more from myself unwilling to step outside of my comfort zone unconsciously relinquishing my freedom. I didn't want to become what I saw: super guard or super prisoner, their own indefinite imprisoner.

I found it humbling that a few super-gangsters looked at me like their key to freedom. Growing up, I thought I could only impress my peers with things like cars and slang. I didn't foresee drive and brains as other ways. A tradition in prison is to give your home address or a family member's home address to your fellow prisoner friends before you are released from prison. That way you can stay in contact and "link-up" in the free world to continue building on whatever it is you all built on in prison. When I got to a medium security prison, I received so many mothers, sisters and baby mother addresses from guys who I only knew for as little as 2 months—vital information to entrust with someone who was practically a stranger.

The "potential" I displayed (I say displayed because I believe more than most of us have it) wasn't the norm in prison, but that doesn't mean I was the exception. There were and still are people who are striving to be as great as they can be. My good friend Salih, practically my brother, attained a bachelor's degree, a master's degree, wrote and published a manifold of books, learned how to write computer code and even learned how to speak German, all while incarcerated. If knowledge is power, he had a lot of power in prison. I would observe how other prisoners would latch on to his every word and accept all of his advice as golden. It's a good thing he doesn't have a tyrant personality. I never witnessed him misuse his influence. I surrounded myself with a handful of people like him.

In hindsight, those affiliations are also what led some of the "less driven" to want to associate/collaborate with me. As one of my fellow prisoners voiced to me, "I want to eat off of your plate. I'm ready to do something different. I wanna do something nice for my moms, buy her a house outside the hood or something."

Though I could relate to his desires, I couldn't accept that type of pressure. The words that kept going through my head were, "Choose your friends, don't let your friends choose you."

There were a couple of things I accepted from my peers. It was common for me to have earplugs in and books spread out on my bed as I studied into the wee hours of the night. An Italian super guard would walk up to the cell I was residing in, peer in and call me "Accanito," an Italian nickname that translates to "Go-Getter." He would tell me that he admired my study habits and was sure to ask me every day I saw him, "Did you learn something today? Good! The future is yours if you want it."

To be recognized as a man in prison instead of number is a bigger deal than you may think. So was being seen as a competitive threat. One super guard was honest enough to tell me that he was impressed with certain skills I had, some of which I mentioned throughout this text. I didn't know we were in competition until he began sharpening his drawing skills. When he discovered that drawing wasn't my thing, he literally waved his latest drawing in my face like a little kid and said, "nah, nah, nah-na-nah, I got a talent you don't have." His potential was so vibrant, it was a shame he wasted so much time as a "correctional" officer. As he chose to compete with me, I felt kind of bad for him.

So what does all of this have to do with S.T.E.M.? Well, S.T.E.M. is what made all of the above so lucid to be.I was reminded through a very peculiar incarcerated engineer that you either have a skill problem or a will problem.

Woody, an old biker guy had been in prison for 38 years at that time, and was losing hope. Being hit at the parole board seven and eight times is abnormal. Every two years he got his hopes up to go home but was denied his freedom. He was about 70 years old, beyond getting in trouble, yet the parole board refused to let him go. He held multiple college degrees and plenty of engineering skills, but the stagnant environment had begun to get the best of him. He started to throw away a lot of his books.

He brought one to me that I would never forget, The Encyclopedia of Engineering. Even though I knew nothing about engineering, he coached to me, "It doesn't matter. You have the ability to learn anything you try to learn. Just keep the book until you feel like learning about engineering."

It was a simple moment, but it made something click in my mind: what he called an "ability to learn" was just my personal approach to learning which I realized that I was taking for granted. He pretty much prompted me to consider how I learn. Something I was never challenged to do before. I tried it.

Once I found out how my mind retains information, I was at a privilege to decide what I wanted to put in it. I wish I could go back and clear this up with anybody who thought I had a different ability than them. I would tell them that we all have "potential" because we all have the ability to learn, but there will be individual approaches and techniques to manifest that ability.

I never fully read that book. Not because couldn't read and understand it, but because I didn't want to. I say all of that to say, I know people who want to learn math but don't know how they learn math, and people who want to learn how to play an instrument but don't know how they learn playing instruments.

I had a "learning advantage" that I never fully appreciated until I received a book that I never fully read. Still, *Engineering* changed my life.

MATHEMATICS

Thinking about that interview, with Dame Dash/
I don't do this for my first name, I do this for my last/
Ain't talking bout the slave masters from the past/
I'm talking bout the ones I'm about to start a new path for/

"Malcolm Little" - Cages to Stages Album

My daughter, Jay, was just three years old when I was first incarcerated back in 2008. I didn't see her again for three more years. She was in Buffalo and I was in a small, lifeless town called Woodbourne. Three-hundred miles between us.

When Jay did come visit me I was nervous. What would she say to me? What wouldn't she say to me? Does she respect me? Does my opinion matter to her? Does she remember how much I loved and cared for her back then? Does any of that stand up to what I've missed out on lately?

The visit started off awkward. My aunt had brought her to see me and we hugged like all fathers and daughters should. But we hadn't had practice in conversing like fathers and daughters should. So instead of addressing her directly, I sat Jay on my lap and asked my aunt about her.

"How was she on the ride here? Did she behave? Did y'all eat? What did y'all eat? blah blah, blah.

But once I finally decided to peek into her mind, and gave her a peek into mine, I realized not only how much we had in common, I found out what she thought of me.

"What's your favorite color?" I asked.

"All of them."

I liked that response. "What's your favorite number?"

"Three," she replied.

"That's weird, mine too. What's your favorite subject?"

"Math," uh-oh, I couldn't relate to her on that one.

I liked math, didn't love it. But I did know this one math trick. "I love math too!" I embellished. "Wanna see a cool trick?" I asked. She nodded fast, hungry to learn.

"What's nine plus nine?"

"Eighteen," she responded swiftly.

"What's one plus eight?"

"Nine," she said slowly, not yet getting it.

"That's cool, right?"

She nodded at me but gave me the look like I was crazy.

"Let's go further. What's eighteen plus eight?"

"Twenty-seven."

"What's two plus seven?"

"Nine," she said with a smirk, finally getting it.

"Twenty-seven plus nine is thirty-six. What's three plus six?"

"Is it nine?" she asked sarcastically. The trick was getting old to her already. But at that moment, something clicked.

"Listen babes, when I come home to you I'll be twenty-seven years old,"

"I already know daddy, and I'll be ...nine!" Jay said excitedly.

"Yes you will, but there's more." This awkward starting visit had just become mathematically divine.

"What's twenty-seven divided by nine babes?"

She shrugged, "We haven't gotten to division yet. I only learned a little from my big cousin."

"That's fine babes, but would you believe me if I told you that twenty-seven divided by nine is three, both of our favorite number?"

Her eyes lit up, "That is a cool trick!"

From that point on, we were totally in-sync. We became more comfortable with each other and realized that we're both goofy, we both love chocolate, we both love to learn and more so, we appreciate each other.

We would continue to do math together through our back-and-forth prison letters. It was so surreal to still be able to be a part of my daughter's education even though I was incarcerated. I couldn't believe how bright she was becoming, and because I was teaching her the multiplication-table and sending more math tricks through the mail every week, she thought I was brilliant. I had actually come across a book that was full of math wonders. One of my professors, Dr. Wolf (one of the most caring teachers who came into prison to teach us), was cool enough to teach me some Vedic math. For about a year straight on Wednesday nights, she would come to the prison and hold pro bono math club showing Vedic math tricks to me and a few other incarcerated men. I would then write my daughter a letter with a few math problems and instructions on how to solve the problem and pull off the trick.

In 2012, while still in Woodbourne "Correctional" Facility, me and about 15 other men walked across a makeshift graduation Stage in the middle of the prison yard. It was a phenomenal event. I was able to invite seven of my family members and friends. I believe 12 showed up. I was asked to give a valedictorian speech by the college staff. I was excited to do it because I knew my family would be there and they would see that I have made lemonade out of my life's lemons. My speech was about the fire and dedication that I and imprisoned men like me possess and how it is fueled by ambition but was ignited by our desire for redemption. I dedicated my speech to my daughter. Seven-year-old Jay's opinion and perspective of me was priority and I needed her to know that. Many people were inspired by the words I spoke that day. Jay had a long six-hour car ride from Buffalo to Woodbourne....so while I was speaking, she was sleeping.

Nonetheless, what started as an awkward prison visit with my daughter transcended into falling in love with mathematics and becoming valedictorian. By researching all kinds of math wonders to send to my daughter, I experienced firsthand how beautiful the subject is. I went on to study Calculus 1, Calculus 2, Calculus 3, Statistics, Probability Theory and even Complex Analysis.

I thought it was cool that learning math more deeply also had a positive effect on my thinking when computer programming. But most significantly, math gave me a new adjective: instead of being her incarcerated father, Jay referred to me as her smart father.

Math changed my life.

Mathematics II

The heat is all I need that's the hood's Geico/

"Hubris" —Cages to Stages Album

I would've never thought that being good at math problems would become a social problem. I plunged face-first into topics like advanced algebra and calculus out of the love for my daughter. I wanted to be able to tutor her throughout high school. But racial stereotypes are what propelled me deeper into math.

Dr. Wolf, that came into teach me and a few other prisoners that were in the college program, had become pretty comfortable around us. Maybe too comfortable.

There were three Black guys in the class, three Latinos, one Asian and one White. One of my friends, 23-year-old Asian guy by the Daniel (the first ever Korean I met who could also speak full blown Spanish), didn't like the grade he received on a quiz. Dr. Wolf initiated a conversation about math and race.

"You did fine on your quiz, but your reaction is so typical. All Asians I've ever taught have these high expectations of yourselves," she expressed.

"Do your Asian students usually perform better than your other students?" one of my Black classmates inquired.

"Not always."

"Do you expect them to?"

Dr. Wolf hesitated. No matter what she said next, she already gave the answer to that question (she eventually said "no").

27

I felt offended. Even worst, I started to see patterns in this professor as well as with others. For example, my homework, quizzes and tests were always criticized more than my Asian counterparts. And that wasn't a terrible thing; I prefer a thorough review of my work. But when I reached a different solution from the teacher, I was immediately told to second guess myself.

"Are you sure this is the right answer?"

"Uhhh..."

However, when my Asian counterparts reached a different solution from the professor, the professor would second guess himself/herself. These racially driven expectations easily became a double-edged sword. On one side, it had the potential to lower my self-confidence and on the other side it actually made my Asian friends complacent and less likely to ask questions that professors "expected" them to already know.

So did it lower my self-esteem? The complete opposite. I made a goal to be recognized by everyone in the class as the top student in the class. I took my professor's set of expectations personal. However, I didn't let my zeal to transcend racial expectations make me overly competitive. I studied ahead so intensively that in class I was grasping abstract concepts seemingly on the fly.

It got to the point that outside of class, my classmates would ask me to lead study groups. Even Daniel. I felt a sense of pride being that I set a goal and reached it. But I also made sure to remain as humble as possible. Daniel didn't have a complex and thus approached me like a man and often asked for help. He was even humble enough to say that I conveyed some topics better than the professor. Him and I actually began to motivate each other and pushed one another to continually study between semesters. We even co-taught math study groups for the new class of students just entering the college-in-prison program. Our synergy was crazy. I remember Dr. Wolf saying how proud she was of us.

By the time the "Discrete Mathematics: Proofs and Fundamentals" course was offered in September 2013. He and I were the only two prisoners that took the class. At this point, I thought I had transcended math and race. I had proved a point to my professor and reached a small goal I set for myself. But race would come back up again.

This time our teacher, Mr. N'daye (Na - Gy) was a Black man from Senegal. The room where we conducted our math class was in an area such that all prisoners could walk by and see exactly what we were working on. People would see the content on the chalkboard and shake their heads in disbelief (Seeing someone prove that the square root of 3 is an irrational number is not an everyday occurrence in prison). But not until an older black guy named Eugene spoke up did I realize that my prior teacher wasn't the only one who had a set of faulty expectations.

Eugene asked, "Is that math y'all learn in that class on Mondays and Wednesdays?"

"Yeah, it is."

"Who is that Black man? He teaching y'all?"

I thought that was pretty apparent since he didn't have the mandatory green pants on like the rest of us.

"Yeah, he's teaching. He's sharp too,"

"Yeah? And it's only two of y'all in the class?"

"Yeah, that isn't easy math we're learning."

"And that Black man is teaching it? Damn, I respect him." He walked away looking pretty astonished.

I laughed to myself considering how we as people sometimes allow our own low self-esteem and lack of self-motivation to put other people into boxes. That alone made me go harder.

I wasn't alone in this thinking. Ryan, a Trinidadian friend of mine, also had an interest in math "just because" he wanted to do what I was doing: breaking down the myth that Blacks aren't good at math (later I'll discuss how my other friends, Jamaica and Salih were also disillusioning the mathematical Blacks naysayers).

Overall, I thought pursuing math would only affect my daughter and I, but it turned out I

was participating in a math "race." I was on a course I didn't voluntarily jump on, but felt compelled to stay on. Math changed my life.

SCIENCE

The judge gave me an offer
For being unlawful/
Embarrassed my family/
And it felt awful/
Was tryna be Marlo, me and young R.O./
Forget the art show, we gambling at the park bro/

"Higher Self" - Cages to Stages Album

Is it ungrateful to turn down a free bachelor's degree? If so, what am I for turning down two free bachelor's degrees?

It was 2011. The college-in-prison initiative I was enrolled in was accepting bachelor's degree applications from students with at least 60 credits. If accepted into the bachelor's program, the student could get a degree in an array of liberal arts studies: Philosophy, Social Science, History, Literature, etc. None of these really fit into my interest at that time, nor did I see a way to immediately monetize such a degree. Yet the idea of attaining a B.A. was attractive.

Not to be misleading, the college program did offer a bachelor's degree in math. But I had not yet fell in love with math and thus didn't have the necessary credits or fundamental knowledge to pursue such a degree. I went on to humbly turn down the B.A. opportunity...sort of humbly (more on that in a moment).

The 2nd degree I turned down about a year later was from another college-in-prison program. This college was offering bachelor's degrees in organizational management. Now this was a lot more appealing to my entrepreneurial mindset at the time.

I have another theory: when someone becomes a felon, his/her mentality is forced into a "recessionary" way of thinking. For example, when a recession hits a country, some economists believe this to be a blessing in disguise because a recession forces the middle class and underclass to be more innovative and take risks they wouldn't usually take when they had a lot more to lose. While businesses and corporations are nervously penny-pinching and downsizing employees, there's usually a surge of entrepreneurs who are willing to take the risks that can dramatically, in a positive manner, affect the economy.

Having a felony can produce this recessionary mindset. One begins to ponder the

improbable; comfort has jumped out of the window; audacity is hugging onto every thought; nothing is taken for granted. Through a subconscious metamorphism, the felon becomes the entrepreneur. The steps are no longer a way to the top. The corporate ladder has been shifted. The elevator is out of order. It's time to design an ambitious technique. Flying is the only option.

I believed that the organizational management degree would be conducive to my future objectives. I put an application in, sent the school a copy of my college transcripts and two weeks later I was accepted. This college program was located in a different facility than the one I was currently residing in. Thus, it would take 2-4 months for the Department of Corrections (DOCS) to transfer me.

If it would have taken 2-4 weeks, I would have a bachelor's in organizational management right now. But 2-4 months? That's a lot of time for my recessionary mindset to consider taking another risk: reject my acceptance into their college program.

And that's what I did. I sent a letter via snail mail asking them to please remove my name from their list and stop any facility transfers with my name on it. I didn't feel ungrateful, but I did regret asking them to put time into considering my application. I hate wasting people's time.

So why did I turn down a bachelor's in organizational management? First you have to understand why I turned down the bachelor's in liberal arts.

At the time when they were accepting B.A. applications, I was six months deep into computer programming. Because the college program was so liberal they considered bringing actual computer programming classes instead of just web development courses. Of course it was possible to order a book and teach myself, but a teacher has the ability to make things so much more comprehensive and learning much more efficient. Since the college program was taking a while to get a teacher in, I found my own.

In 2011, while still at Woodbourne "Correctional Facility," I met a wiseman.; let's call him Jamaica. He had been incarcerated since the early 1990s. Many people call him a genius but after being around him for just a few months, I found out first hand that he's a product of pure hard and diligent work. Jamaica deserves credit for the foundation of my computer programming knowledge. He was the one who helped me expand my skill-set beyond building websites and introduced me to what insiders call the "backend." Learning how to code in prison brought me a sense of comfort, confidence and optimism.

During B.A. enrollment season, a few of us (minus Jamaica who already had a bachelor's in mathematics) decided to make a very strong suggestion to the Director of the college program: bring in a bachelor's degree for Computer Science. We made a pact with each other: if they wouldn't bring in the Computer Science we wouldn't put in our applications.

The strategy flopped! The Director didn't accept the proposal because a Computer Science degree, he claimed, involved "working on robots," and DOCS wasn't having that.

"So there's no way you can get a bachelor's in Comp. Sci. without taking that one course in Robotics?" I inquired.

"Yes, that is the case." (I did some research and found out that a robotics course doesn't make or break a computer scientist).

The three of us had made a pact and I was sticking to it. As we got up to leave the meeting with the Director, he said to one of my classmates,

"Can I have a word with you?" And with that, our pact was out of the window. My classmate was another victim of the old "divide and conquer" strategy.

Ten minutes later my classmate came out of the room and told me that the Director said he would not take our "pact" personal as long as we at least put in our applications.

I did some research and found out through a staff member of the college that if I submitted the application, and it was accepted, I was committed to be moved to the prison where the B.A. program was being implemented at. Not in my plans. I chose to stay in Woodbourne C.F. where the computers were and chose not to put in the application.

A year later, when the organizational management degree was offered to me, I was now 18 months deep into computer programming. It was amazing to me that I had enough knowledge to think up an idea and actually build it. And like everyone with ideas, I thought mine were game changers. Thus, during that two-four month period of waiting to be transferred to the facility that offered the organizational management degree, I came up with a website and mobile app idea that I really, really wanted to build so that I can just get straight into marketing when I get released. However, I couldn't build the website and app in two-four months. Even worse, I wouldn't have access to computer programming software in the facility I would be transferred to. So I took a risk. I turned down a second free bachelor's degree.

From the outside looking, I probably looked ungrateful and indecisive. But on the inside, I heard my intuition loud and clear. I followed my heart. The same heart that had been seduced by my new-found passion and what would successfully become my way out of the hood.

Science changed my life.

Re-Entry

I was released from on November 18th, 2014. My mother and step-father drove me from Woodbourne to Buffalo. Then my brother drove me from Buffalo to Florida. I was able to see my daughter in Buffalo for a few hours since I was obligated by the Probation department to be in Florida within 48 hours. It was hard leaving her again, but it was the middle of the school year and I knew she would be moving to florida in 7 months. That gave me 7 months to get my life in order and build a foundation for her in Florida. At that time I wasn't in a relationship, but her mother - Gina - wanted to rekindle what we started about 10 years earlier as teenagers. I invited her to move down with no guarantees we would be together. I told her we could try it out and see where it went.

I was dead broke living out of my brother's house. I'm so lucky for him, otherwise I'd have to stay at a homeless shelter. By the time Gina and Jay moved down in July of 2015, I had already found a job at a tech company, launched a 501 (c) (3) charitable foundation and incorporated a software development firm with my cousin Greg and my homeboy Craig. After 7 years in prison, it seemed as if I didn't sleep for my first 7 months home.

I immersed myself into the new world I was living in and acclimated quickly. No one wondered if I was incarcerated for the past 7 years. I showed no signs of it and before I knew it, I was surpassing people. Not in the sense of being better than someone, but in regards to accolades, income, connections and positive impact. I was no longer a victim to the Prison Bell Theory. I had unlocked my mental cage years ago and now that I was out of my physical cage, there was nowhere to go but up.

Gina and Jay began helping out immediately. Gina was planning events for the charity and Jay was by my side learning how to code. While I was incarcerated, Gina gave birth to a enthusiastic boy - Jayden. Because his father was not in his life, Gina brought him to Florida as well. I always wanted a son. I accepted him with open arms.

In less than a year of being released from the worst place I had ever been, I was blessed with a family, a non-profit team, a tech team and a great support system. Once I got out of my own way, I realized all that life had to offer me. Everything I have today was there the whole time.

JOURNAL ENTRY
7/11/2018

Ten years ago today, I was a different person. I woke up, spent about 50% of my life-savings on a worthless new outfit which included shorts, a shirt and a pair of Nikes. I got dressed and ever so casually slipped a loaded 357 into the waist of my jeans. I was a different type of person. I was ready to die. I was ready to kill. Today I'm neither. Today I'm more forgiving. I'm more patient. I'm more understanding. I'm more human. Instead of combating every confrontation that comes my way, I aim to diffuse them.

10 years ago today I had no idea I only had a few more hours to do what I wanted to as a free man because the next 12 years of my life would be spent in the notorious U.S. prison system: seven years of which would be in prison, five on Parole.

Ten years ago today, I had no idea that 10 years later I would be the Founder and CTO of Atlas Digital Group. That I would be the Co-Founder, Creator and Executive Director of Photo Patch Foundation. That I would be teaching people how to code online. That I would be the father to three beautiful children. That I would be co-teaching a robotics programming class with my 13 year old daughter. That I would be in love with the girl I fell in love with at a boys and girls club when we were just boys and girls. That I would be exploring and developing augmented and virtual reality with my cousin and my brother. That I would be speaking on different platforms and Stages across the country about the hardest days of my life and how I used those days to become the best father, son, brother, cousin, nephew, uncle, colleague and friend anyone could ask for.

I worked hard to repair what was broken in me. Was it my parents' divorce? Was it watching all of my friends and cousins die at a young age? Was it leaving my daughter without a father at the age of three? Was it the trauma, heartache, and confusion I put my family through when they had to put their lives on pause to help me transition from a free man to an enslaved prisoner? I think it was a combination of them all. I was tired of knowing right from wrong and steady choosing wrong. I wanted to stop cheating, taking shortcuts, and being so lackadaisical about life. Coming to that realization while in prison is what helped me escape my mental prison. As I rap on "K.E.Y." from the album, Karma is real.

If Karma's everything/
I'll get her a wedding ring/
I used to move that ecstasy/
Now I move like X and King/

I realized that my thoughts and actions of today will boomerang in the future. I have to be intentional today about what I want tomorrow.

I'm shedding tears as I write this because it feels good to have a journey. So many people have lost their lives before their story was truly finished. I was given a second chance and I feel like I did not take it for granted. It feels good. Really good. I can only imagine how many other people have felt this same way and how many people would like to feel this same way.

I was released from physical prison in November 2014. I was released from my mental prison in 2008, just a few months after being in county prison. I said I would come home and do it right this time. And I have. A lot of people thought it was "jail talk." But that's why my daughter's lyrics on "Can't Believe" are some prolific to me:

They ain't see it/
I believed it/
Everything I said I do, I achieved it/
Everything I said I do, I achieved it/
And I'm still achieving/

Everything I said I wanted to do, I strived for it. I showed honest intent and 4th quarter effort. I'm proud of who I am, where I've been, where I'm at, and where I'm going.

8 Keys That Unlocked My Cage

I wouldn't say that I was born into a broken household. Granted, my mother and father divorced when I was just a year old, but in hindsight, having a step-mother and step-father only gave me access to more love, guidance and resources. That is if they were willing to give it, and I willing to receive. The former wasn't a problem. However, seeds were obviously planted and as years went by, I began to realize the Keys that had been deposited into my subconscious.

I'll break down just a few here as I feel S.T.E.M. has often helped extract and give the opportunity to apply those Keys.

#1 Practice P.I.E.

If prison is good at anything, it's time management. Everything is on a strict schedule at all times. I took that same mentality with me when I left prison. Being incarcerated I truly understood the value of a minute. How much can get done in a minute, or not get done in a minute. Once I was free again, my plate quickly filled up: back with my family, working a day job, running three businesses and making music. I had to make sure to maintain a healthy balance of everything.

Instead of getting overwhelmed with life, I have consistently emphasized mentality of thinking and executing in increments. I call this the P.I.E. Technique - Prioritize in Increments and Execute. The goal is always to get 100% done of everything I have committed to. However, I can only complete 1% at a time and that's what I focus on. So I break all of my commitments down into goals and then break the goals into incremental tasks. I found that I get triple the amount of work done this way. A big reason why I can get so much done (besides my family sacrificing so much time with me) is because the time I used to spend pondering and deciding on what to do next, now can be used for execution time.

To this day I keep a detailed to-do lists (there are a ton of apps and websites to help you manage this) and I prioritize that list on a weekly, daily and nightly basis. The key is, once the day is rolling, I only focus on what is at the top of that list. Once it's done, check it off and move on to the next thing. We all know how easy it is for our list to get huge. So what, keeping adding to your list, stay focused on priorities and continue reminding yourself that everything will get done in due time, but at this moment it's not worth the stress.

If something on that list is stressing you out, move it to the top of the lists, complete it and move on with your life. Keep that incrementality. Learn more on CagesToStages.com/PIE-Techniquie

#2 Self-Humble

I once read, "If you don't humble yourself, the universe will do it for you". Whenever I need some humbling, I open up a math book. Mathematics is a universe in itself. If you ever feel like a know it all, the infinite infinities of Mathematics will show you otherwise.

Math is a bittersweet subject to learn. One second you feel like you're making some progress, and then you turn the page and you're in a new domain, a new dimension, a new discovery—to your mind at least.

And such is life. In math we turn the page and see how much we don't know, while in life we can turn the corner and see how much we don't know. When I open a math book, I make a conscious decision to open my mind and prepare to learn something new. This is something I strive to do in my everyday life: open my mind to the world—the people, the cultures, the mentalities, the creatures, nature and the surrounding magnificent sky—and I humbly learn.

In one way or another, the wisest people have all said the same thing: "A man who knows something, knows that he knows nothing at all."

#3 Give Back

This Key is probably closest to my heart; my experiences with S.T.E.M. have given me opportunities to put it in application. I appreciate the fact that I have the knowhow to build websites and mobile apps, so much so, I feel it necessary to build products that I believe to be of use to society. I want my skills to make other people's lives if not the best, better. One of my favorite tracks on the Cages to Stages Album is "Stages." The first verse starts with:

I would trade the money for the power/
I would trade the power for the love/

The lack of not being able to see my daughter or get letters and pictures from her is what's sparked my most compassionate idea. While still incarcerated, I begin working on a website that would allow kids to send pictures to their parents in prison. I called it Photo Patch. From experience I knew photos could patch wounds of loneliness, regret and fear. I envisioned youth being able to send letters and pictures directly from their phone or computer, to their parents in prison; all for free. I wanted youth to be able to reach out to their mom or dad at any moment, without postal mail being in the way.

In 2014 I was released and I immediately launched Photo Patch Foundation as a 501(c)(3) nonprofit. I assembled a team which included my friend Craig, whom I was incarcerated with, my cousin Greg (who can relate to having a parent in prison) and even my daughter Jay. In fact, after teaching her some fundamentals of coding and programming, Jay built the mobile app for Photo Patch. I had been teaching her how to code for the last 2 years. To this day, Photo patch has helped connect thousands youth to their parents in prison (www.photopatch.org).

Giving back is a part of my life. I often get to exercise it when I'm teaching or tutoring my peers, family and friends in music, math or science. I even have the pleasure of volunteering my time mentoring incarcerated youth with my friend Laura at a local juvenile facility. Suncoast Kids Place, a Tampa based non-profit that specializes in working with troubled youth, reached out and asked if we'd be interested. Giving back to at-risk youth was a no brainer for me.

Besides clean coding, one thing my first computer scientist teacher, Jamaica, imparted upon me was the process of perpetual teaching, or what some people call "each-one-teach-one."

He would say, "If I teach you how to do this, it's your duty to teach others."

I would have paid thousands of dollars for the knowledge he held, but perpetual teaching is all he ever asked for in return. I still feel indebted to him and many others who have taken time to teach me. If I ever get the opportunity to help you, you can thank me by passing it on.

#5 Debug Often

If you're a programmer you've probably spent so many hours debugging that those hours can accumulate to years. But programmer or not, everybody has done some debugging, especially those striving to become a better person. Debugging is just a manner of finding defects (or bugs) that are making some process inefficient. I became very good at debugging my computer code, quickly finding the syntax and logical problems. So I asked myself, "If I started debugging my life," which is just one long process in itself, "what problems would I find?"

Incarcerated, I would often find time to sit in that prison cell and examine many of my old experiences: fist-fights, suspensions, financial losses, dropping out of college and many of my embarrassing moments as well. As it turned out, besides the long-term effects of systemic poverty and oppression in communities of color, the second biggest bug in my life was usually me. Whether it was my stubborn pride, youthful slickness, my toxic habits or carelessness, most situations in my life didn't have to play out the way they did. If I would have known myself better—more significantly. If I would have known certain situations were caused by my "buggy'" behavior—I could have prevented a lot of losses. Not just money, but relationships as well. I could have recognized my faults and apologized.

Whereas debugging is usually a stressful process when coding, I realized it can be therapeutic in my day-to-day life. Before going to bed at night, I play the day through my head and debug each "event." Being able to debug computer code has made me a better all-around problem solver.

#5 Keep an Optimistic Mind

I have to give credit to S.T.E.M. for reminding me to keep an open mind. Growing up, I never thought I would watch a Star Trek production, or any sci-fi for that matter. But as I found out how much our brilliant physicists, mathematicians, astrologists, chemists and engineers have discovered, the truth of science fiction became apparent: sci-fi wouldn't be fiction for too much longer. I now strive to always keep an open-mind to new ideas and seek understanding before being dismissive.

The knowledge I accumulated from studying S.T.E.M. allowed me to keep an open mind about my getting a job upon being released from prison. So many people miss out on job opportunities because they check the box that says, "Have you ever been convicted of a felony?" I didn't want to be one of those people. I would've rather been the person that didn't check the box, got the job and risked being pulled into the supervisor's office six months later after a random background check. But hey, maybe six months into the job they would appreciate my work ethic and understand why I lied on the application. Maybe they wouldn't. Either way, S.T.E.M. gave me a skill-set to be proud of a skillset that many companies can utilize. S.T.E.M. kept me optimistic about the idea that some people will chose my present and my future over my history.

Upon release, I did in fact lie on the first job application I filled out. It was for a budding tech startup based in south Florida. I often considered bringing up my felony conviction, but I had a family to provide for. I chose to risk it. Deep down I knew I wasn't a threat to the company or any of the employees, so I had no regret taking the risk. I excelled at the job but for some reason my conscience was eating me.

Paranoid, I fell into a pattern. I found myself working at tech companies for about a year before I would start looking for a new job. I realized how much easier it was to get a new job, once you already have a job. There was one time I was applying for a Software Engineer position and I didn't get it. The tech team and human resources put me through a thorough 3-part interview which I was told I passed. However, as the hiring manager told me face-to-face, "There's something I just can't put my finger on." And he denied me the job. I walked out of that office so confused, wishing he would have at least lied to me about what I did wrong. Instead I was left to believe he was profiling me even though I was well qualified. I stayed optimistic and had a higher paying job for the same position within a few weeks.

After a few years of job hopping, I finally was offered a position at really cool and blossoming tech startup. An associate who had become a good friend of mine, Jason, had just raised $2 million from investors for his online reputation management company. In the past, he had volunteered for my non-profit, Photo Patch Foundation, so he was aware of my journey from Cages to Stages. His startup was growing fast, getting national attention in fact. Him and the lead developer, Mike, called me and basically asked if I wanted the job. No application, no box to check or leave unchecked. He was so open minded about hiring me, I wondered for months if he remembered that I told him I had a felony conviction. But he did. And he never once judged me. I still appreciate and study him to this day. When you are trying to master something, you admire the people who already have.

#6 Intentionally Practice Discipline

We've all probably heard the phrase, "If you don't use it, you'll lose it." Taking Calculus 1, Calculus 2 and Calculus 3 are what magnified that truth to me. In between the semesters that I took Calculus 1 and Calculus 2, I didn't continue to study the important concepts I learned. So during the Calculus 2 class, I didn't pick up on new concepts so fast because I had trouble recalling the concepts that those new ones were built upon.

I didn't like this idea of having to go back and learn something twice. So between the semester I took Calc 2 and Calc 3, I made sure to exercise my math skills at least a few times a week. As I went further into some higher math, I increased my out-of-class studying time. Eventually I set a schedule: every morning, Monday through Friday, at 6:30 I'd wake up to do at least a half-hour of mathematics. Setting a goal like that made me exercise my discipline to not only push myself to get out of bed, but it also disciplined me to go to bed at a decent hour which I had become horrible at.

Thanks to this strategy, I now retain a lot more knowledge. Furthermore, discipline is needed in all facets of life, not just math. But like math, if I don't consciously and continuously practice discipline, I'll lose it.

#7 Embrace Discomfort

S.T.E.M. didn't actually magnify this Key for me; but it did give me an opportunity to exercise it. The importance of this concept first hit home while reading Drs. Randall Pinkett and Jeffrey Robinson's book, "Black Faces, White Places" which essentially gives practical advice on being Black while attaining excellence in life. They meticulously discuss maintaining a high self-esteem, a strong sense of identity, the power of a diverse network, amongst other topics.

My favorite part of the book is the section where the authors suggest the importance of discomfort:

> It is only when we seek experiences that bring about a healthy level of discomfort—those experiences that challenge us to do things we normally would not do—and when we are exposed to differences—perspectives,places, people, and possibilities that are dissimilar from the ones we are accustomed to—that we grow and develop...Broad exposure and diverse experiences that push you further into our growth zone must happen deliberately, because they are key to your future success. Top performers are not just comfortable with discomfort—they actively seek discomfort. They are constantly in search of ways to grow and improve upon their abilities.

In their book, Drs. Pinkett and Robinson gave a "visual depiction of growth and development" which you can see in Figure 1.

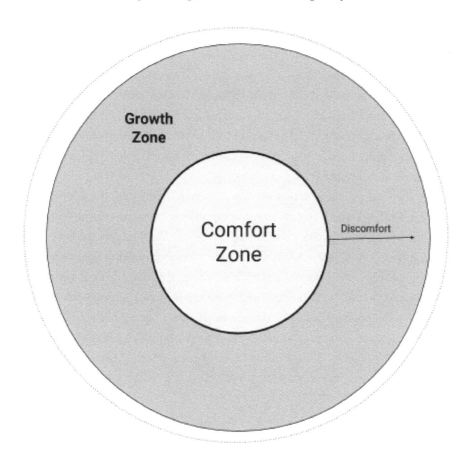

Figure 1

"The beauty of the diagram is that there is always the possibility of drawing additional circles (see the dotted circle). As your comfort zone becomes larger, your growth zone can also become larger. The possibilities—for you and our society—are endless."

This wasn't the first time I heard this, but it resonated with me differently this time and I almost immediately understood why. Still incarcerated, I had just about five months left before I would re-enter society. One of my friends, Jamaica, offered to teach a Complex Analysis class to myself and a couple other guys. None of us declined even though I thought about doing so since I had a couple projects (a mobile app and a novel) that I wanted to finish within the next five months. But I refused to turn down the opportunity.

Two weeks into the class, however, I was regretting it. The way my mind picks up math concepts involve a process that takes significant time, practice and repetition: at least three hours of studying every day, but usually more. If I don't get three hours each day, then I'll be kind of lost in class which means I'll have a ton of questions. I don't mind asking questions, I mind asking the most questions. So at times I caught myself nodding my head (I should have been shaking my head) when Professor Jamaica asked if we all understood the concept he was teaching.

To be truthful, there was more to why I hesitated to ask questions: I soon recognized that I was insecure about being the most mathematically immature person in the room. Jamaica had his bachelor's in Mathematics and my Korean friend, Sky, was a couple of credits away from having his as well. Then there was Salih who had a bachelor's in Literature, a Master's in Ministry and due to all of the Mathematic courses he took, for credit, he practically had a bachelor's in Mathematics (The college-in-prison program allowed him to keep taking math courses, but for some reason wouldn't let him actually get the bachelor's degree). To make me more uncomfortable, Jamaica allowed one of the college's professors to sit in on the class: Dr. Wolf, a freaking Math Doctor.

While taking this course, I began reading Black Faces, White Places, so I immediately related the discomfort the authors spoke about to my current circumstances: the same thing that was making me uncomfortable and insecure is exactly what should have made me grow.

It was a simple yet illuminating manifestation. It was no secret that I didn't have more mathematical knowledge than anyone in the room. In fact, I was at least 10 years younger than everyone in the room. Logically speaking, I should have been asking the most questions in the room. Once I took this logic to class and began firing away with questions, I progressed much faster. And my classmates and teacher actually voiced this to me! It's like they were waiting for me to ask what I thought of as "basic" questions, but what they saw as "fundamental" questions.

To this day I strive to hold the Growth/Discomfort Diagram in my mind. I seek more moments when I'm the least smart person in the room because those moments of discomfort are beautiful opportunities to grow.

#8 Dream Bigger

Neil deGrasse Tyson. Nikola Tesla. Mae C. Jemison. Stephen Hawking. Percy Lavon Julian. Albert Einstein. All of these people are known for dreaming big. If I could say one piece of advice to anyone in a Cage, it would be: dream big and then dream bigger.

While incarcerated, I had over a dozen black and white notebooks jam packed with ideas. I thought I would implement them all. Of course I was being very irrational. However, the audacity I displayed to even consider accomplishing so much payed off in the long run. Like they say, 'Shoot for the sky, that way if you miss you'll still be amongst the Stars." I may have set some unrealistic goals but striving for them put me into some amazing situations. I have some great friends whom I met as prisoners but when I call them or see them on social media, I see no resemblances of that part of their past. My friend Brandon now has his own clothing brand and store, Farbridge. My friend Intell launched uswear which sells unique motivational and uplifting clothing. My friend Johnathan, in less than 3 years has opened a Nostrand Station Bar and Lounge in Brooklyn. And I can go on and on. As I said many times before, I'm not the exception, I'm an example.

For those of you still in Cages (mental or physical) let me share with you how passion and audacity lead us to Los Angeles where we made a ton of connections within five days. My younger brother, Zach, was helping us build the west coast branch for Photo Patch Foundation. He was able to connect and form some awesome partnerships with organizations like Place 4 Grace, P.O.P.S. The Club, Sister Inmate, Unlock Tomorrow and Words Uncaged to name a few.

So I remember we were invited by our friend Jessica from Words Uncaged / Unlocked Tomorrow to be apart of their hackathon. It costs us about $4000 to fly out there and survive for those five days. And we had no intentions on making any money so that $4000 was more of a long-term investment than anything. My cousin Greg, my brother Zack and my daughter Jay attended the event. The challenge was to build a new solution for people coming from prison, also known as "re-entry." There are services that specialize in this already, but there aren't enough and most of them just don't know what a former prisoner really needs to bounce back, be successful and not recidivate. We had the experience and the technological knowledge to put together some great By attending that hackathon, and winning may I add, we made a ton of connections and built a bunch of relationships.

The project my team came up with was a 3-prong program called Hatch. To reduce the chances of someone recidivating, we would start working with the inmate while incarcerated. They would have to take our one-year program which would be an intensive deep dive in coding, photography or social services. Upon release they would be mandated to come live in our Hatch Incubator where they would continue learning their chosen skill set but also have a paid internship at one of our partner's companies. 50% of their income would be put into a savings account and would be matched at the end of the program by one of our donors. Then there would be a "Hatch App" to help you manage your savings, track milestones, view job boards and even apply for jobs. The program sounded utopian and audacious but that's why the judges loved it.

We met people from Headspace, which is a multimillion-dollar meditation-based tech company (one of my favorite apps at that time). We even got invited to their office. Before we got to the office everyone was told about Jay and the app she built. So needless to say as we got our tour we were approached by a bunch of people congratulating her on her accomplishment and thanking her for her community service. It was truly humbling, and kind of surreal when I thought about this whole thing was invented while in prison.

At the hackathon, we also met people from Snapchat, Cal State University, and Ideo as well, a huge design firm based out of California. The relationships we cultivated that week are still alive to this day. We were able to put our computer science hats on and really help build a real-world solution for reentry. It was a really fun hackathon. But we weren't done. Because we still were going to be in LA for a couple more days we made it our business to try to meet some more cool people as well. I remember we stopped by A.R.C. (Anti Recidivism Coalition) to see if we could meet the Executive Director at the time Shaka Senghor. He had done about 19 years in prison and was on a similar journey of Cages to Stages. For me it was special meeting him that day, because we didn't have an invite to his office. Instead my team and I showed up and asked for a tour and our boldness combined with our unique nonprofit open up the door for us to have an impromptu meeting with Chaka. Once he heard about what photo patch was and how Jay build the app, he was all the way on board. He even told Jay he will be her mentor. Shaka is also the best-selling author of Writing My Wrongs. He gave Jay his book, signed it and encouraged her to continue writing as well. It was truly a surreal day. Jay and I would go on to read his book while traveling on flights leaving LA.

While reading his book I learned a lot about atonement and Redemption. On a layover flight from New York City to Buffalo New York, I finally found the courage to tell my daughter the full story of why I went to prison in 2008. I told her every detail, which I haven't even told in this memoir. That moment was everything to me—a cage I still had yet to unlock.

Reading Shaka's Writing My Wrongs helped see how important it is to own your past, and let go of any regret. The intentional thoughts, decisions and actions I made in prison led us to building a mobile app which opened up the door for us to attend a Hackathon, do a fireside chat, visit a huge startup, meet a bunch of intelligent and conscious people and even do a 360 video interview with VRX Connect. Merging our tech skills with our community passion has been one of the best things I've ever done.

Dream big my friends, and then dream bigger. As my bro Zach religiously believes, "Anything is Possible." Project yourself upon this world, not the other way around.

If I can do it, you can do it.

FINAL WORDS

I would hate for this small book to be misconstrued as the "correctional" system at work, because it didn't work. DOCS—the Department of Corruption—is still broken. I worked, I sought, I observed, I learned, I took risks and sacrificed.

In 2009, two weeks into me being transferred to a state prison from a county jail, in some dingy discreet hallway, six-eight super-guards had me surrounded. One of the guards was upset that I was talking "too loud" 10 minutes earlier. As the guard walked off, another prisoner inquired about what the guard said to me.

I coolly brushed it off, "Nothing much, he's just trying to intimidate me." Ten minutes later I was escorted to the discrete hallway. It was obvious that the super guard over heard me. Now, equipped with an eight-man squad he was overdoing the intimidation.

Long story short, he wanted to fight. He also wanted his co-workers there in case I got the best of him. I quickly weighed the odds and thought it best not to fight him. So when he flicked a lit cigarette at my face, I dodged it. When he put his hands up, ready to spar, I kept my hands down. And when he swung at me, I easily bobbed his 55-year-old fist (he could have been my grandfather).

What I didn't dodge was the sneak punch to the back of my head. One of his buddies was either getting antsy or didn't like the way I was dancing around his partner.

The punch dazed me, not enough to drop me to the floor, but I fell anyway. Staying on my feet would have only enticed the rest of them to sneak in blows as well. Instead, when I frizzed up on the dusty floor, the 55-year-old pounced on top of me.

It didn't last long. He hit me in places so as not to leave bruises. Yet, I'm conscious that I could have died back then. And I'm not certain that I would make the same decision not to fight back today.

I say all that to say this: If I would have defended myself against those six-eight guards, my life would be different today. I would've had to do at least five years in "the box" and ended up charged with a new criminal felony (assaulting an officer).

The unfortunate part is, at this very moment, there is another male or female prisoner who is a discrete hallway about to get jumped by some guards. The system is beyond broken. There's a lack of staff supervision, a lack of care for rehabilitation, a lack of humanness and unfortunately, a lack of public concern.

Besides the aforementioned altercation with the super-guards and a few other minor incidents, I can't overstate how grateful (and probably lucky) I was that so much played out in my favor. One day I just decided I wanted to pursue a S.T.E.M. career and I happened to be in a unique prison that allowed a privately funded program to operate a college-in-prison initiative. Unfortunately, not many incarcerated Americans have the same opportunity. Of the 2 million or so prisoners, a journey akin to mine is extremely unlikely to occur more than a very small percentage of the time. Doesn't it make you wonder what is meant by Criminal Justice?

Coming Soon

Cages to Stages: How Meditation Changed My Life

Cages to Stages: How Music Changed My Life

Cages to Stages II - The Album

CPSIA information can be obtained
at www.ICGtesting.com
Printed in the USA
LVHW051728160519
618108LV00013B/864

9 780692 173282